WORLD ABOUT US
NUCLEAR WASTE

B. GARDINER

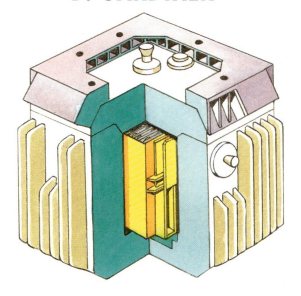

GLOUCESTER PRESS
London·New York·Toronto·Sydney

© Aladdin Books Ltd 1992

Designed and produced by
Aladdin Books Ltd
28 Percy Street
London W1P 9FF

First published in
Great Britain in 1992 by
Franklin Watts Ltd
96 Leonard Street
London EC2A 4RH

Design: David West
Children's
Book Design
Designer: John Kelly
Editor: Fiona Robertson
Illustrator: Mike Lacy
Consultant: Peter Roche,
Greenpeace

ISBN 0 7496 0745 9

Printed in Belgium
All rights reserved

A CIP catalogue record for this
book is available from the
British Library.

Contents

Nuclear radiation
4
Uranium mining
6
Inside a reactor
8
Moving fuel rods
10
Re-processing
12
Liquid waste
14
Long-term disposal
16
Low-level waste
18
Deep burial
20
De-commissioning
22
Accidents will happen
24
What will we do?
26
Fact file
28
Glossary
31
Index
32

Introduction

Thousands of tonnes of uranium are used in nuclear power stations and bomb factories. The nuclear waste that is left over will remain radioactive for thousands of years. Most of it is far too dangerous to go near. Large amounts of nuclear waste already exist, and more is being made all the time. Safer ways of storing this nuclear waste must be found if we are to protect future generations from its harmful effects.

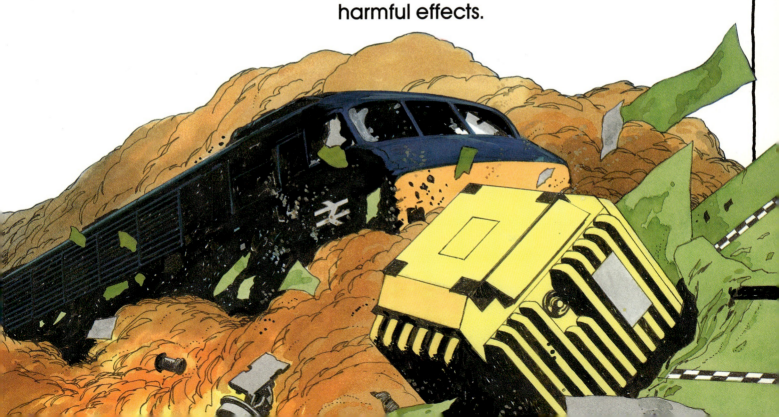

Nuclear radiation

Everything is made of atoms, which are very tiny particles. At the centre of each atom is a nucleus. The nucleus of an ordinary atom stays in one piece. But the nucleus of a radioactive atom is different. A small piece of the nucleus can suddenly break off, and shoot out at tremendous speed. These fast-moving particles are nuclear radiation. Some radioactive nuclei can also be split deliberately, to release energy for making electricity or bombs.

Neutron

Krypton-92

Uranium-235

Neutron

Barium-141

Neutron

When the nucleus of a uranium atom is split, more neutrons are released.

The three types of nuclear radiation are alpha and beta particles, and gamma rays. Each has different strengths of penetration (see below).

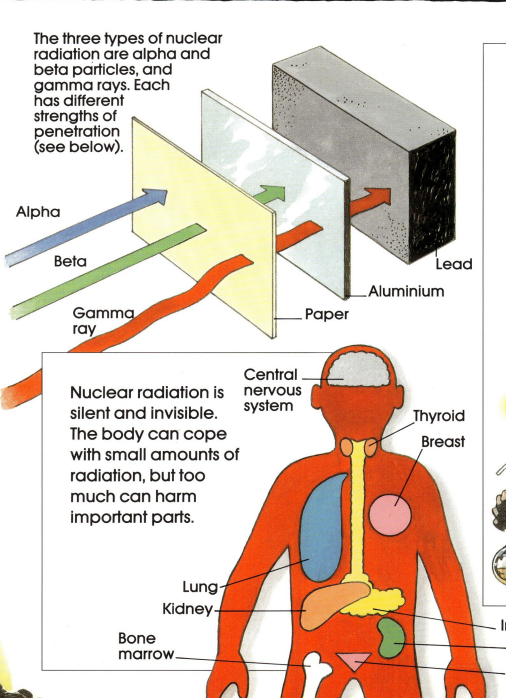

Alpha

Beta

Gamma ray

Paper

Aluminium

Lead

Nuclear radiation is silent and invisible. The body can cope with small amounts of radiation, but too much can harm important parts.

Central nervous system

Thyroid

Breast

Lung

Kidney

Bone marrow

Intestine

Kidney

Reproductive organs

Natural radiation

In 1898 Marie and Pierre Curie discovered radium while studying rocks from a mine. They detected alpha particles. Many miners developed lung cancer from breathing in radioactive dust.

Uranium mining

The fuel used in most nuclear power stations is uranium. Uranium is found in rock in very small quantities. When it is mined, tonnes of rock are crushed to sand, and then soaked in powerful acids to extract the uranium. However, the rock also contains radium and radon, both of which are naturally radioactive. The miners are carefully monitored to ensure they are not exposed to too much radiation over a long period of time.

Modern uranium mines are very big, and use both open-cast (surface) and underground mining. Using huge cranes and dumper trucks, the miners dig up hundreds of tonnes of rock to get one tonne of uranium.

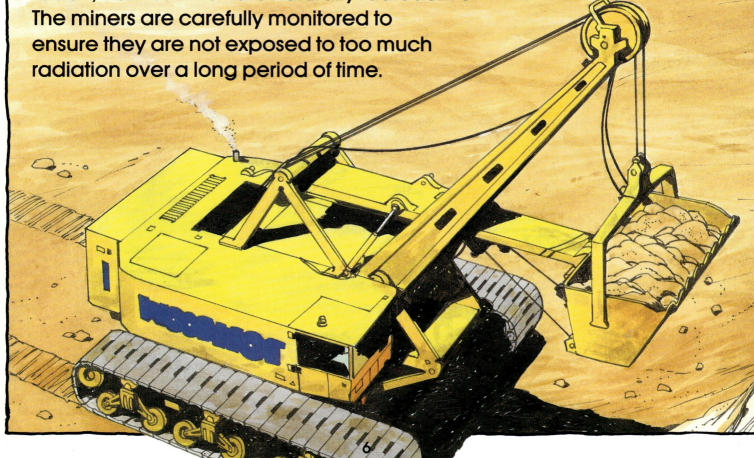

6

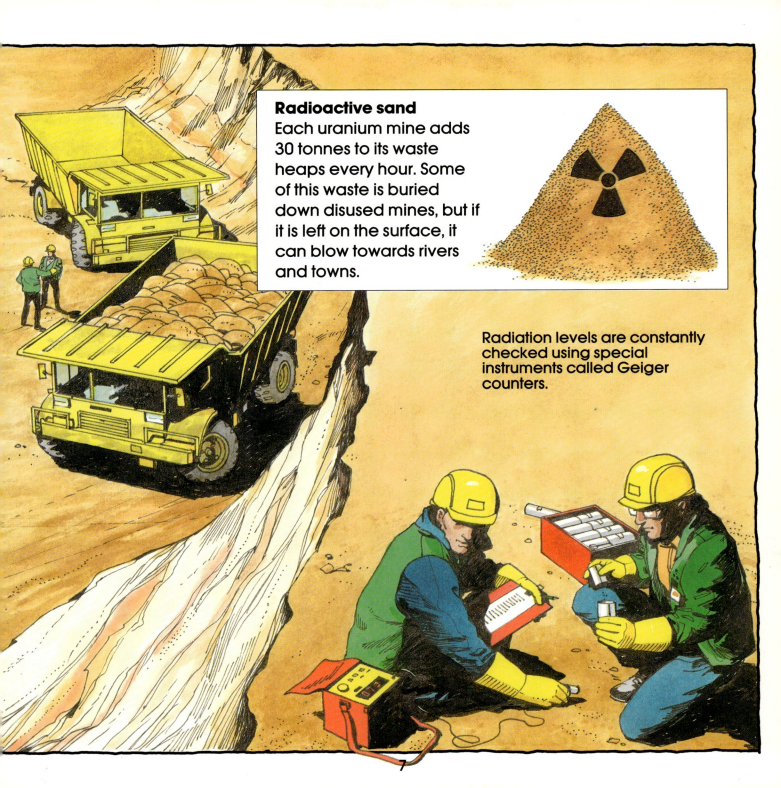

Radioactive sand

Each uranium mine adds 30 tonnes to its waste heaps every hour. Some of this waste is buried down disused mines, but if it is left on the surface, it can blow towards rivers and towns.

Radiation levels are constantly checked using special instruments called Geiger counters.

Inside a reactor

Fresh uranium rods, which are not yet dangerous, go into the reactor of a nuclear power station. Deep inside, the uranium atoms are blasted by neutrons and broken up. More neutrons are set free and the reactor gets hotter and very radioactive. The heat is used to make steam to drive an electric generator. After a few years, the fuel rods are replaced with new ones. The old rods are dangerously radioactive.

The mined uranium ore is purified and turned into fuel pellets that make up the reactor's fuel rods. At this point it is safe to handle the uranium.

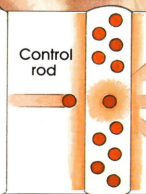

Controlled reaction
Millions of neutrons are flying about in the reactor, breaking up the uranium atoms. The reactor would melt if control rods didn't stop some of the neutrons.

The uranium atoms release heat when they are split.

The control rods catch some neutrons to prevent overheating.

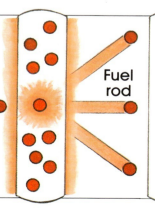

Fuel rod

Control rod

After the fuel rods have been used in the reactor they are too dangerous even to look at without a protective screen. From this point on, they must be handled by remote control.

9

Moving fuel rods

The used fuel rods from the reactor are so radioactive that they produce their own heat. Even after several months in a cooling pond they are still too dangerous to handle. Remote-control cranes lift them into a large metal cask. The lid is sealed and the cask is loaded onto a railway wagon. From here the old fuel rods are sent either to a nuclear waste store, or to the re-processing factory.

To find out whether the nuclear fuel casks are strong enough, a special test was arranged. With film cameras running, a railway engine was sent at full speed towards a cask lying on the track.

Lid

Fuel rods

Inside the cask
The radioactivity in the fuel rods keeps producing more heat, so the cask is filled with water to keep them cool. The walls of the cask are very thick, to stop the dangerous nuclear radiation from escaping.

The railway engine was
destroyed in the test, but the
cask stayed in one piece,
proving that radioactive
material is unlikely to
leak out.

Cask survives impact

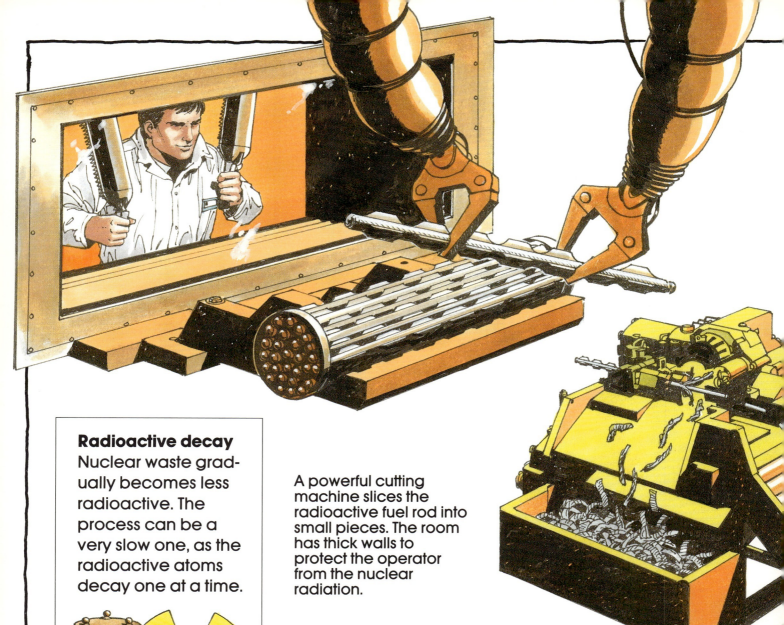

Radioactive decay
Nuclear waste gradually becomes less radioactive. The process can be a very slow one, as the radioactive atoms decay one at a time.

A powerful cutting machine slices the radioactive fuel rod into small pieces. The room has thick walls to protect the operator from the nuclear radiation.

The waste tubing from around the fuel rod is also radioactive, and is collected separately. Everything is done by remote control.

Re-processing

The old fuel rods contain some plutonium and uranium which could be used in the future. Behind thick concrete walls, a machine chops up the radioactive rods and dissolves them in nitric acid. The operator looks through a window tank full of a special liquid which absorbs the gamma rays. Once the plutonium and uranium have been separated, the remaining liquid waste is so radioactive that it has to be cooled in tanks for 50 years.

Re-processing is very expensive and is not considered essential in some countries, because they do not need more plutonium. In addition, radioactivity released into the air or sea during re-processing can be avoided if the rods are simply stored.

The pieces of fuel rod are passed through various chemical baths, to separate the uranium and plutonium.

The remaining liquid is pumped away and stored in huge tanks.

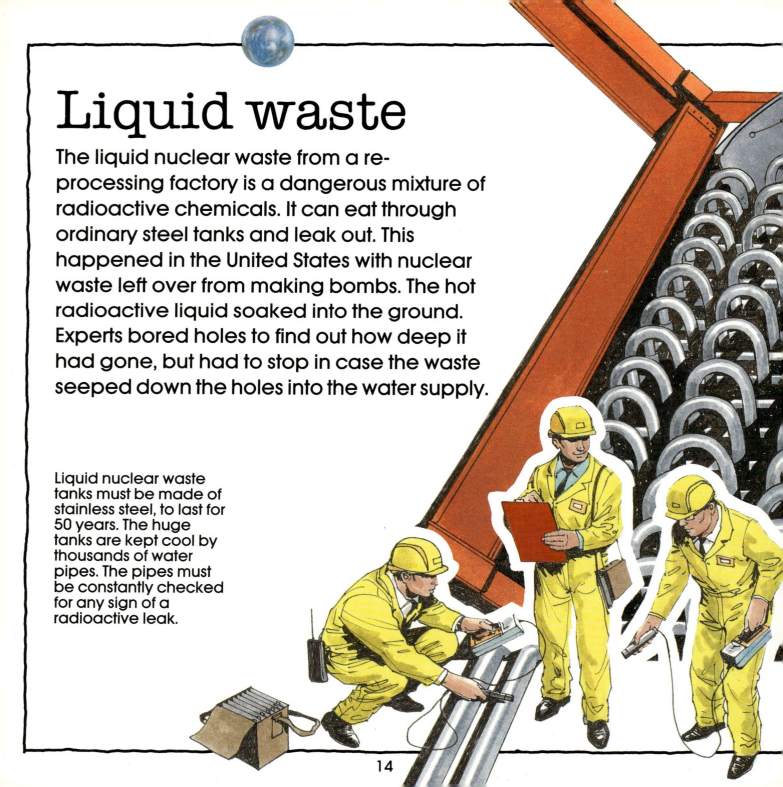

Liquid waste

The liquid nuclear waste from a re-processing factory is a dangerous mixture of radioactive chemicals. It can eat through ordinary steel tanks and leak out. This happened in the United States with nuclear waste left over from making bombs. The hot radioactive liquid soaked into the ground. Experts bored holes to find out how deep it had gone, but had to stop in case the waste seeped down the holes into the water supply.

Liquid nuclear waste tanks must be made of stainless steel, to last for 50 years. The huge tanks are kept cool by thousands of water pipes. The pipes must be constantly checked for any sign of a radioactive leak.

14

Cooling pipes

Atom-bomb waste
Re-processing was developed during the Second World War to extract plutonium for the first atom bombs. But the liquid waste produced is also highly radioactive.

Long-term disposal

Nuclear waste from power stations and re-processing factories remains radioactive for thousands of years. The problem of storing nuclear waste for such a long time has still to be fully solved. To stop liquid waste from leaking through the storage tanks, it will have to be taken out and turned into solid blocks. One way is to melt nuclear waste and glass together. The liquid glass is poured into steel drums and left to solidify.

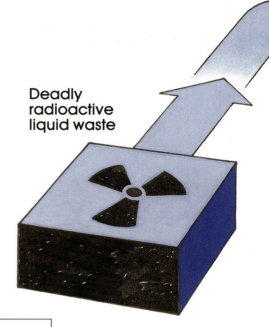

Deadly radioactive liquid waste

How safe is glass?
Glass does not last for ever. After many years the radioactivity makes it brittle. Special types of glass have been made for nuclear waste, but there is no way of knowing whether they will last long enough.

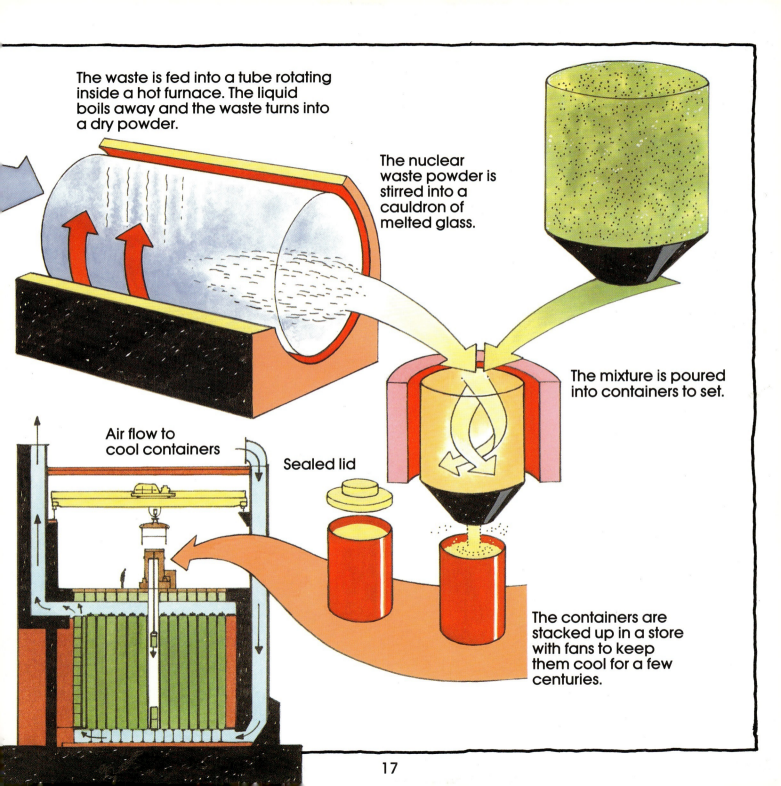

The waste is fed into a tube rotating inside a hot furnace. The liquid boils away and the waste turns into a dry powder.

The nuclear waste powder is stirred into a cauldron of melted glass.

The mixture is poured into containers to set.

Air flow to cool containers

Sealed lid

The containers are stacked up in a store with fans to keep them cool for a few centuries.

17

Low-level waste

As well as the highly radioactive waste from nuclear reactors, there is an even bigger quantity of rubbish which is only slightly radioactive, called low-level waste. Clothing, brushes and towels used by nuclear engineers are packed into drums and buried in shallow trenches. Some countries have built specially-designed concrete storage sites to deal with the large quantities of low-level waste.

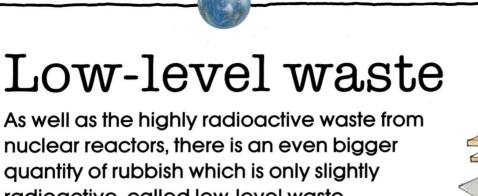

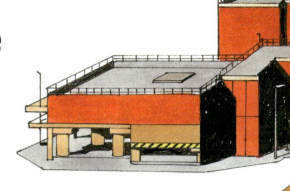

One of the dangers of burying low-level waste is that it could leak into the surrounding area and contaminate local water supplies.

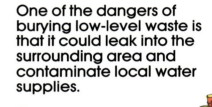

Low-level waste comes not only from nuclear power stations and re-processing factories, but also from hospitals and research laboratories.

Radioactivity cannot be destroyed by fire or chemicals. It slowly becomes less radioactive as the radioactive atoms die away, or decay.

For many years, drums of low-level waste were dumped in the ocean, where they fell to the bottom. Liquid low-level waste is still poured directly into the sea.

Some people feel that the waste should be stored on the surface, so that any leaks can be dealt with immediately.

The sites for deep burial must be carefully chosen so that radioactive gas cannot escape into the environment.

Deep burial

We are making more nuclear waste all the time. The safest way to deal with it is to bury it in specially constructed chambers deep underground. Because nuclear waste has a lifetime of thousands of years, the waste must be stored in steel caverns, which will be sealed up with concrete. The rocks in which it is buried must be hard, like granite, to prevent any cracking. But even the safest methods of deep burial cannot be guaranteed against events like earthquakes in the future.

Most people don't want a nuclear waste dump near their home. But it has to go somewhere.

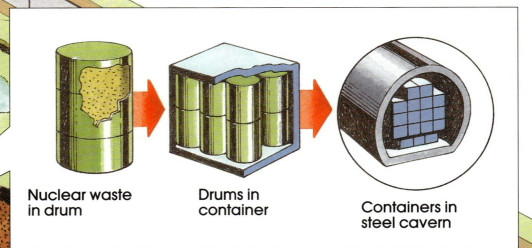

Nuclear waste in drum

Drums in container

Containers in steel cavern

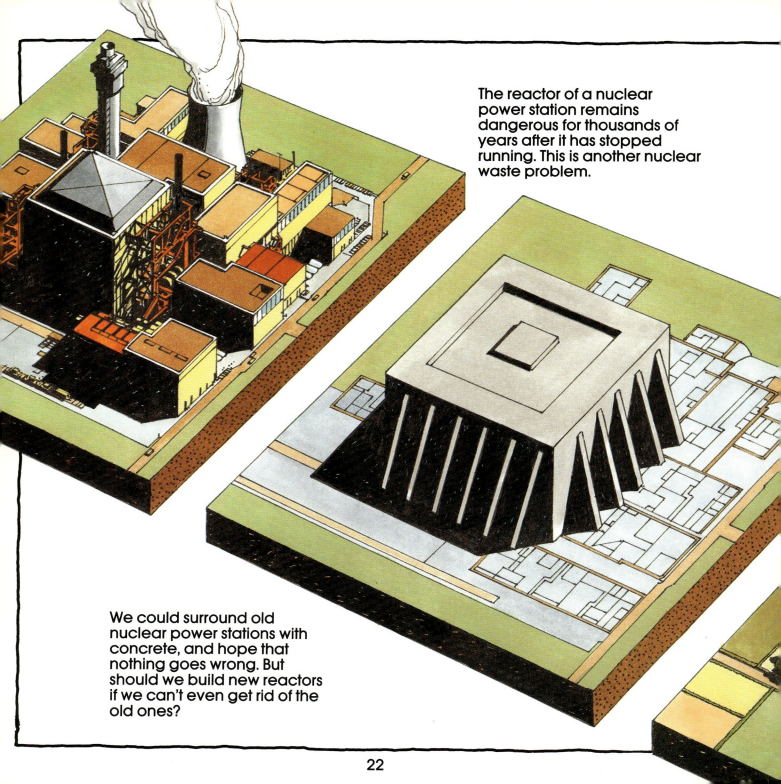

The reactor of a nuclear power station remains dangerous for thousands of years after it has stopped running. This is another nuclear waste problem.

We could surround old nuclear power stations with concrete, and hope that nothing goes wrong. But should we build new reactors if we can't even get rid of the old ones?

De-commissioning

A nuclear power station only lasts about forty years. After it has been switched off, the de-commissioning work begins. This means making it safe. The nuclear reactor must either be sealed up safely or taken away. It is extremely difficult to take an old reactor to pieces. Even if the used fuel rods are removed, many tonnes of highly radioactive waste remain. The simple answer is to build a thick concrete shell round it.

The best solution would be to build new equipment to cut up the radioactive core by remote control and dispose of it safely.

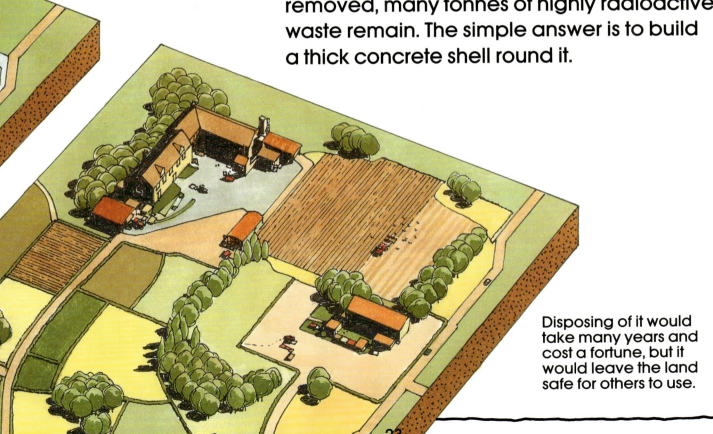

Disposing of it would take many years and cost a fortune, but it would leave the land safe for others to use.

Accidents will happen

There have been serious accidents in nuclear reactors all over the world. The usual problem is a broken pump or a leak in the cooling system. All reactors have emergency cooling systems, but even the best systems can fail, sometimes due to human error. The worst nuclear accident was at Chernobyl. They were trying out a new safety idea, but it didn't work. The reactor overheated. Then it exploded, caught fire, and melted.

Nuclear meltdown
Huge amounts of heat are produced in a nuclear power station. If the cooling systems fail, the reactor overheats. This makes the fuel inside melt down through the concrete floor of the containment building, contaminating the surrounding area.

Many people died at Chernobyl. Thousands had to flee from their homes to escape from the huge cloud of radioactive smoke.

In the days following the explosion, a radioactive cloud wafted across Europe, polluting food crops and pastures with a thin layer of nuclear waste.

Area affected by Chernobyl accident

Radiation path in first week

Wind changes on day 6

In the future, people will not tolerate nuclear waste. Our energy will come instead from the wind and the waves, and from the Sun which drives them.

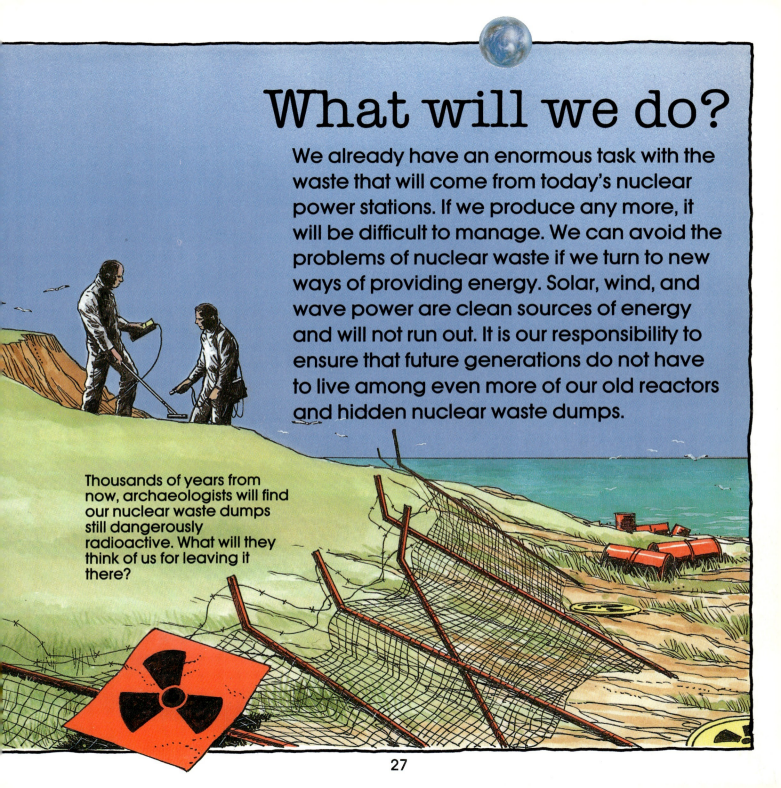

What will we do?

We already have an enormous task with the waste that will come from today's nuclear power stations. If we produce any more, it will be difficult to manage. We can avoid the problems of nuclear waste if we turn to new ways of providing energy. Solar, wind, and wave power are clean sources of energy and will not run out. It is our responsibility to ensure that future generations do not have to live among even more of our old reactors and hidden nuclear waste dumps.

Thousands of years from now, archaeologists will find our nuclear waste dumps still dangerously radioactive. What will they think of us for leaving it there?

Fact file

A Japanese nuclear-powered ship leaked radioactivity on its first voyage. The crew tried to repair the leak with rice and old socks, but without success. For six weeks the ship was not even allowed to enter harbour. It never did work properly and eventually had to be scrapped at enormous cost.

The nuclear reactor at Three Mile Island in the United States went badly wrong in 1979. A series of mechanical failures and human mistakes combined to prevent cooling water reaching the reactor core. Heat built up in the reactor, making the core overheat. Part of the uranium fuel melted, releasing radioactivity into the air.

When nuclear fuel rods are re-processed, krypton gas is released. Re-processing factories simply let the radioactive krypton escape. There is now so much in the air that people who use cylinders of concentrated liquid air are exposed to nuclear radiation from the concentrated krypton.

Most satellites get their energy from the Sun, but a few are powered by radioactive heat. There is no room in a satellite for a nuclear reactor, so it uses the heat from a block of plutonium. When the satellite re-enters the atmosphere, it scatters nuclear waste on the ground. Fortunately, this only happens very rarely.

After the Second World War, two nuclear bombs were tested by exploding them on Bikini Island in the Pacific Ocean. Radioactive mud soon filled the lagoon. After 25 years the islanders were allowed back, but it was unsafe. Even the crabs were radioactive. Nobody lives there now.

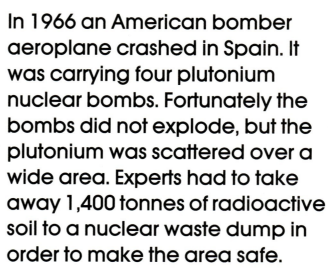

In 1966 an American bomber aeroplane crashed in Spain. It was carrying four plutonium nuclear bombs. Fortunately the bombs did not explode, but the plutonium was scattered over a wide area. Experts had to take away 1,400 tonnes of radioactive soil to a nuclear waste dump in order to make the area safe.

Glossary

De-commissioning
Taking a nuclear reactor apart at the end of its useful life, and tidying up the land afterwards.

Neutron
One of the tiny particles that make up the nucleus of an atom. Neutrons are released when a nucleus is split.

Nuclear radiation
Fast particles shooting out when nuclei break up. Too much nuclear radiation is dangerous to life.

Nuclear reactor
A block of uranium fuel rods in which heat is released by splitting uranium nuclei. A reactor also contains control rods and cooling pipes.

Nuclei
More than one nucleus.

Nucleus
The central part of an atom. It consists of protons and neutrons.

Plutonium
A radioactive metal which can only be made inside a nuclear reactor. Plutonium is mainly used in nuclear bombs.

Radioactive
Producing nuclear radiation.

Re-processing
Dissolving old uranium fuel rods in acid to extract the plutonium and unused uranium.

Index

A
accidents 24, 25, 26, 30
alternative energy 26, 27

B
bombs 14, 15, 30
burying 18, 20, 21

C
Chernobyl 24, 25
cooling systems 24, 28

D
de-commissioning 22, 23, 31

F
fuel rods 8-10, 12, 13, 23, 29

G
glass 16, 17

L
liquid waste 14-16, 19

long-term disposal 16, 17
low-level waste 18, 19

M
meltdown 24
mining 6, 7

P
plutonium 13, 15, 29-31
power stations 8, 9, 16, 22, 23, 27

R
radiation 4, 5, 31
radioactive decay 12, 19
re-processing 10, 13-16, 31
reactors 8-10, 22-24, 31

U
uranium 4, 6, 7, 13

W
waste stores 10, 13, 16-18, 27

PRINTED IN BELGIUM BY

INTERNATIONAL BOOK PRODUCTION